Beyond the Mask:

Exposing the unseen

By: Chancey Jacob Hall

Cover Art: *Jacob Wrestling With the Angel*, 1856-61 (Oil over pen and ink on tracing paper; mounted on canvas and backed with linen), Eugène Delacroix, Saint-Sulpice, Paris, France.

To all those who have hurt and helped heal
me.
I couldn't have done it without you.

Preface. Don't skip... I know you want to but it's important you don't.

I want to start this collection by saying that these writings were never intended to be shared. When I began my writing journey, it served as an outlet for expressing my innermost thoughts and feelings without fear of judgment. Over time, I have come to appreciate the value of letting others in, despite the fear it may bring. I have seen the benefits of sharing my thoughts, feelings, and struggles with others. Hence why I am now releasing them. My heart behind this text is based upon my own experiences and trying to break a mold I have witnessed and had formed. With that being said, here's some background!

Throughout my journey, I have witnessed and experienced the masks worn by those within the church. Many followers of God, myself included, hide behind these masks, presenting a facade to the world while concealing our true struggles and vulnerabilities. The church can sometimes feel like a place where everyone is expected

to have it all together, but the reality is that many of us are hurting and broken, desperately trying to maintain an image of perfection. However, I want to clarify that not everyone who professes Christianity is like this. I have been blessed with a community that allows vulnerability and mutual support.

I have seen firsthand the damage that this pretense can cause. It creates an environment where people feel isolated in their pain, believing they are the only ones struggling. I have experienced this isolation myself, feeling the pressure to conform to an image that did not reflect my true self. It took a long time for me to understand that this facade was not only harming me but also preventing me from experiencing genuine healing and connection.

When I finally removed my mask, I was able to begin my personal healing process.

Exposing my hidden wounds and admitting my vulnerabilities allowed me to confront

the pain that had been festering beneath the surface. It was not an easy journey, but it was a necessary one. By bringing my struggles into the light, I found that I was no longer bound by them. The things that once held power over me began to lose their grip, and I started to experience true freedom.

In sharing these writings, I am taking off my mask and showing people the struggles and thoughts of someone who follows the teachings of Jesus. In opening my writings to others, I have found freedom and witnessed others feel less alone. My hope and prayer are that, through these pages, you may also see that you are not alone in your struggles. Whether you are a person of faith or someone pursuing healing, I believe that the themes of struggle, healing, and redemption are universal. We all wear masks of some kind, hiding parts of ourselves that we fear others will not accept. But I have learned that there is incredible power in vulnerability.

I also would like to take time to explain the cover painting as it has developed great meaning in my life. It is a visual

representation of this journey I have embarked on throughout the years I have been learning and pursuing God. It depicts the wrestling match between Jacob and God

(the story comes out of Genesis 32, Christian or not. I suggest reading the story. It will greatly impact the way you view God.) A powerful symbol of the struggle we all face in our faith and in our lives. This image resonates deeply with me because it encapsulates the essence of my writings. Much like Jacob, I have found myself wrestling with God, questioning Him, and seeking answers in the midst of my pain. These writings were born out of those struggles, moments of deep anguish, and profound questioning.

Lastly, through the process of putting this all together, I cry tears of joy for the first time as I have come to see the beauty in everything I have experienced. I hope one day you are able to experience it also.

Here's to your journey,
Chancey Jacob Hall <3

Trigger Warning

Before you start, I want to let you know that this book discusses topics of death, suicide, and sexual assault. If these subjects are tough for you, be cautious as you proceed. I encourage you to reach out to someone you trust. I understand that it might not seem like it right now, and these words may feel hollow because I once felt that way too, but it truly does get better, my friend. Keep pushing forward; don't give up. You are incredibly valuable.

Beyond the Mask

CONTENTS

Section I: The Struggle Behind the Mask

Beyond the Mask

I've been who everyone needed me to be for so long, I don't remember who I really am.

Then again, how can I even know the real me if I don't even know who that is?

How can I find something when I don't even know what I'm searching for?

Will someone ever be there to catch my tears, or will it always be my pillow? Will I ever know the feeling of lasting comfort, or will that, too, be something I search for endlessly, only to end up lost?

Some days I feel peace; others I feel like
dying.
Some days I feel invincible; others I want to
hide under a rock and never return.
Is this the battle of life? Or is it just me?
Is this what makes us beautiful?
Is this what is meant by a beautiful tragedy?

I'm tired of this back and forth in my mind.
When will it end?

One moment was all it took. One picture was noticed on a screen. In an instant, everything got worse.

What I first felt goes beyond the reach of language.

Beyond the Mask

As I laid there unconscious, next to the toilet with my pants around my ankles, you decided that your sexual desires were more important than my innocence or even my body. You were supposed to be my friend. I trusted you, and in that vulnerable moment, you chose to betray that trust in the most horrific way.

What made it even more devastating was that you professed to be a Christian. Your faith was supposed to be a guiding light, a moral compass, yet you chose to commit an act so contrary to the values you claimed to uphold. How could someone who called themselves a follower of Christ and made sure others knew it do something so horrendous?

The image of that night haunts me, a stark reminder of the moment my sense of safety and trust was shattered. I had believed in our friendship, confided in you, and never imagined you would take advantage of my vulnerability. You prioritized your twisted desires over my humanity, over the sanctity of our bond.

In that instant, you transformed from a friend into a perpetrator, and my life was irrevocably altered. Your actions spoke volumes about who you truly are, and they left me grappling with the aftermath, struggling to reclaim my sense of self and my ability to trust others.

Worse, it led me into a deep struggle with anger towards God, questioning how He could allow such a betrayal to happen and why someone who professed to follow Him could act in such a way.

The journey has been long and difficult, but I have discovered solace and strength through my faith. God allowed me to experience my righteous anger, affirming that it was natural to feel such emotions because He too was angry at the injustice. However, He did not let that anger consume me. Instead, He lifted the burden from my shoulders, enabling me to find forgiveness. Even now, I cannot fully explain how this transformation occurred.

I forgive you. Not because your actions were justifiable, but because clinging to pain and anger keeps me trapped in that moment. Forgiveness is my way of breaking free from the chains of the past, embracing a future filled with hope and resilience that God desires for me. Despite the darkness of that experience, I refuse to let it define me. I am more than the sum of your actions.

They ask if I'm okay but are not prepared for the real answer. That I fantasize about death yet marvel at life. That I question my very existence yet know I am loved and seen by God. That I cry more than I laugh and smile but don't mind because, for once, I'm feeling something. No, I'm not alright. I'm not sure if I ever will be, but I'll still tell you I'm fine.

If only they took a second
To see what i've been through,
To understand the healing,
And strength it took to be who I am now.

The pain you caused felt like a cold winter, one without the comfort or sheer notion that you know the heat will be with you again. Going to bed was the only escape, only to wake up to again be accompanied by the shrieking cold that seems to never change. You want to get help, but you're frozen. Frozen in a pain that has been the end of most. Will I ever feel the heat again? Will I survive?

The pen became my knife, the paper my skin.
In seeking a release, I chose the ink's
permanence over the scars within.

Why do I romanticize misery? Aren't I tired of feeling empty? There is marvelous beauty in the healing of brokenness, but self-torture offers no such beauty. Do I truly believe I am unworthy of happiness or the joys life has to offer? Or am I simply afraid of leaving behind what I know, thus remaining imprisoned within myself?

I feel as if I am trapped. This paper is my only way to release. No one is ready for the darkness that I hold inside, not even I.

Some days, I question why I can feel so
deeply yet also have the ability to shut
feelings off. Is it because I needed to save
myself after attempting to kill myself? I've
never truly considered the weight of that
until now. I did try to kill myself. Maybe, just
maybe, God allows me to feel deeply to
remind me of the joy I can experience
because I've known such profound darkness.
But why does happiness flee quicker than
sadness and anger? I seek this answer, but
will I find it, or do I need to look deeper?
How deep must I search to feel lasting joy?

I retreat to sleep, hoping for a different reality, but worry that it will never become more than a dream.

My mind is a battlefield with countless battles; I can't tell who's winning anymore. Will this war ever end? Surely it must, since the enemy is me. The war between self and mind, a battle never forgotten.

All I've ever wanted was to feel loved.

I've realized that I ask "what if" more often than usual, as if seeking a sense of control. However, I can't waste my life being curious about what could have been or what I might have changed. I need to process my experiences and move on. Dwelling on the past often traps me in a deep pit of sorrow and despair—emotions I desperately want to escape, yet my actions seem to anchor me there.

I desperately want to feel comfortable in my own skin, but I can't remember a time when I ever did. How do I feel something I've never known, a comfort that feels so impossibly out of reach?

What I would give to live a carefree life. One where I do not worry as much, don't overthink, or care about my perception. What I would do to be free—free of myself. But for now, I serve a life sentence. The jail cell: my mind.

Forever to be
Enslaved by
Anxious, unbearable,
Rampant thoughts.

Sometimes, I feel as if I am the subject of a cruel joke played by all of humanity. Why does such a feeling even exist? Am I a slave to my psyche, or is it the harshness of an unfortunate reality I must bear? If it is all in my head, why can I never seem to escape? Have I formed a prison in which I am meant to remain forever? Or is what I view as a prison actually a refuge, created to shield me from the unbearable suffering of my perceived reality, yet transformed into something else entirely?

Will I forever be searching for the love I never received as a child? Or perhaps it wasn't entirely absent, but instead, dissolved into a vast void of nothingness, leaving me to chase shadows of what could have been.

Am I homesick for something I have only experienced in my imagination?

I've found that I tend to ask more questions than rest in the marvelous things I've been shown and brought through. I believe this stems from my childhood. A child is supposed to be curious, carefree, and innocent—experiences that were stolen from me.

My mind often leans toward anger because of the years of healing I've had to pursue, healing from things that were never my fault. This journey has brought much despair. I was exposed to life's deepest complexities before I could even comprehend what had happened. What I would give to have my innocence returned.

Why did no one stand guard over me?

Was I not worth it?

Section II: Unmasking

Beyond the Mask

Beyond the Mask

I want to take off my mask,
But who will they see?
A monster,
Or the child
Who was forced to put it on?

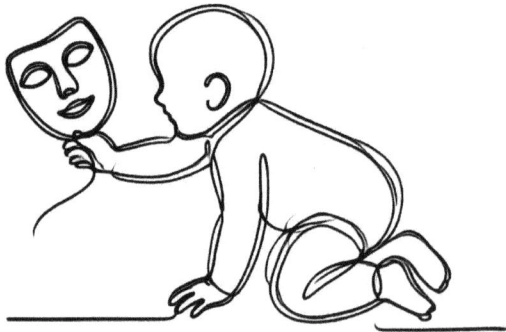

I fear the judgment of unveiled truth,
Yet crave the freedom it promises.
For in the depths of my soul,
I know there's more than what they've
known.

Beyond the Mask

Every facade, a piece of my shield,
A barrier to the pain I concealed,
Removing each, with trembling hands,
I face the world as my soul expands.

When I am alone, everything I've hidden is finally revealed. What I see even scares me; perhaps that's why I've kept it concealed from others for so long.

My existence has been a reflection of moments that should never have been. How do I uncover who I truly am when I've always been a product of my past?

As the day comes to an end,
I take off the mask.
I lay my head, a tear rushing down my cheek,
Questioning if they will ever accept the real
me.

Another morning, another mask. This time, it weighs more than ever before. Will there come a day when I cannot bear to lift it anymore?

I tried to put on my mask today but couldn't.
Could things be changing?

Is this how it was always meant to be?

I refuse to wear this mask any longer; I'm
ready to know who I am without it.

I think I'm okay with being misunderstood by those who don't truly try to know me. Shedding the need for approval, I realize that assumptions made without the curiosity to understand who I truly am say more about you than about me. Their assumptions don't define me. God knows who I am, and that's all that matters.

As the beliefs built to protect me are broken
down, or what I thought as to.
I see everything I was supposed to be,
A child, able to express
Without the fear of being contained.

Beyond the Mask

As I showed you parts of me no one has seen,
You embraced every part,
Seeing the beauty in my true self,
Not just who you wanted me to be.

By shedding this disguise,
I reclaim my voice and my story.
Freed from the expectations
Of who you and everyone else thought I
should be.

Beyond the Mask

Exposing everything I hid,
I grow into who I'm meant to be,
Not the person others created
Or who I thought I'd be forever.

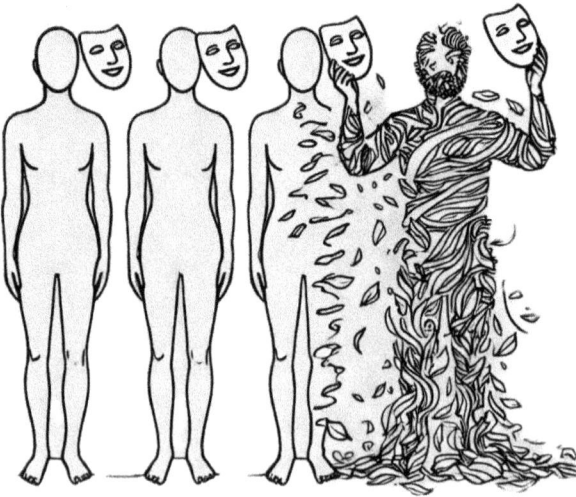

Beyond the Mask

Section III: Reflections and Realizations Laid Bare

Beyond the Mask

My life is filled with contradictions. I'm breathing, which means I'm alive, but do I ever truly allow myself to live? I often spend my life searching for meaning , like a journey through an uncharted forest without any guidance—no map, no compass, no GPS. In my desperate attempts to find where I should be, I have often overlooked the beauty that surrounds me.

Is life simple, or is it hard?
Is it simple, yet do I make it hard?
Is it because I secretly don't want it to be
simple?
I say I do, yet I make it more difficult.
Things aren't always as complicated as I
make them out to be.
Do I create complexity because I'm scared to
face the simple truth?

What I would give to be like a child again. Not a worry besides what is the next game we will play. What I would give to go back and have a childhood as such. The envy to have what would have truly been a joyful childhood. But yet I dreamed of growing old because I thought things would be better and I could escape. I couldn't have been more wrong. Is this the pain of regret or a realization that we don't recognize joy until it's too late?

I wonder if things will always stay the same mentally. I know they won't, due to the sobering fact that everything is bound to change. My real worry is whether my mentality or views will just shift to a different variation of the same thing. Do things ever truly get better, or do I just learn to cope more easily or bury things deeper within myself?

I don't think I chose to be this way; it's a result of my childhood or other traumatic experiences. I feel pain, just like everyone else; sadly, none of us are excused from it. Yet, I go through life without telling a soul, carrying pain I was never meant to bear alone. Where is the beauty in withholding? When I share my experiences, I connect with others and help free them too; it gives me the chance to find joy—a wish many have, but few ever experience.

Courage is a funny thing to me. It can change my life forever in a positive way, but the lack of it has the potential to ruin it. A lack of courage reveals the power I give to fear. I've come to realize that fear is one of the worst things I can hold onto. It has the ability to withhold me from many things I was meant to enjoy. Yet, just seconds of courage can change so much—the courage to talk to that person, to forgive, to have that difficult conversation, to pursue healing, to pray. The list goes on. Courage is something I have always lacked but am now finding the value in pursuing. I will never know what could happen if I don't try. I've learned it's better to try and maybe fail or get hurt than to live with the pain of regret.

Maybe, just maybe. All this pain and anger is built up from the grief I now experience of having to grow up too soon.

Beyond the Mask

Your mistakes robbed me of half my life.

I should have never had to parent you, that was your job.

How can you give life to something and only care for it when it offers you something in return?

I have had enough of this torture. When will you recognize that you too need to own up to your actions. Then again you never have so why should I expect it now.

You know I guess "sorry" isn't in your vocabulary. Then again that would require empathy, which you don't have, at least not to me. Why would I expect more from you?

I hear how you tell them how proud you are of me, it would be nice to hear it from you and not them.

They fail to see the struggle I faced to make the decision to no longer speak to you. I wrestled with guilt and societal expectations. But I knew that maintaining contact only prolonged my suffering. Embracing the silence and distance was my way of reclaiming my life.

In the quiet moments alone, I reflected on the years of pain and manipulation. Realizing that my worth was not tied to your approval was liberating. Each day, I discover more of who I am without your shadow looming over me. The decision to distance myself was not just an act of self-preservation, but a courageous step towards my own healing and growth.

I am learning to forgive myself for the times I stayed silent, and I find strength in acknowledging my own needs and setting boundaries that should have always been there. This journey has taught me that sometimes, the bravest thing we can do is to walk away from what harms us.

Beyond the Mask

You installed ideas and thoughts inside my
brain that were never meant to be there.
But here I am, stuck healing from something
that wasn't my fault, again.

Your words, like seeds, planted doubt and
fear,
Growing weeds in the garden of my mind,
Choking the blooms of my identity,
Twisting my reality into knots of confusion.

I dig deep, uprooting these invasive
thoughts,
Tenderly tending to the wounds left behind,
Nurturing the fragile sprouts of my true self,
Longing for the day when my mind will be
mine again.

It's a slow process, this healing,
Like mending a broken wing,
But I am patient, I am strong,
I will fly once more.

Like I was always meant to.

This healing journey I have embarked on is
treacherous yet blissful.
I have begun to find beauty in things I once
thought Satan had conquered.
It is shockingly brilliant what can happen
when I open my heart and mind to the things
of God.
I have come to realize that life is not a
tragedy but a marvelous journey we must all
undertake.
A journey where tragedy is made whole
through the reshaping of our minds,
A process the Creator has designed us to
embrace.

Every person carries a different story, each as unique as the individual who lives it. We long for our stories to be seen and heard, yet fear often keeps us silent. Perhaps we are afraid because we know all too well the judgment we ourselves cast. We wonder why others don't open up, berating them for silently suffering while claiming to be a "safe and judgment-free zone." But do our actions truly reflect that promise?

We hold back because we replay moments of past judgment—both the judgments we've faced and the ones we've inflicted. We become prisoners of our own fears and prejudices, trapped in a cycle of silence and judgment. In the end, it's our own actions, our own judgments, that become our demise.

The sky had a softness to it, a gentle quality that brought a sense of ease to my mind with its subtle yet breathtakingly beautiful colors. Perhaps the most subtle things tend to be the most beautiful. I have never seen a sky like this; I thought such beauty could only exist in paintings or in my imagination. Maybe I am being shown that what I once believed to be only a dream can indeed become reality.

For in that moment,
I could have been stranded at sea
and been fully at peace.

I am ready to write a story beyond sadness.

.

In my vast array of despair I have begun to reflect and recognize the beauty that can be found in the darkest of places.

Section IV: Echoes of Love and Heartbreak

Beyond the Mask

It wasn't just the way she put her hand in mine when I was anxious or the way she spoke to me. It was everything in between. She made me feel the way I always knew I should. But fear took hold and snatched her away. What a waste of something that could have been so beautiful.

I wish my mind would focus more on the love she made me feel instead of the heartbreak that was caused.

I'm always going to love you, and that's what hurts the most. No matter how much time passes or how far apart we are, my heart will always ache for you. The love we shared brought me the greatest joy, but now it brings the deepest pain. Loving you was the most natural thing in the world, but living without you feels like an endless struggle. The permanence of my love for you is a bittersweet reminder of what we had and what can never be again.

I read a quote by an unknown writer that said, "And I wondered what it was like to be chosen. I was never chosen; I was a maybe, a probably, sometimes even a definitely. But never the one."

This is how she made me feel in the end. Yet, I still chose to love and hope for her. Maybe I was blind and just wanted my dream of romance, where both let go and completely let their emotions run wild for one another, to come true. The problem is, my dream is just that—a dream. Not real, only in my mind. Will someone ever show me this isn't a dream? Or will I forever be stuck chasing something that may not even exist?

Letting go of you was letting go of something I could never seem to form. I don't know how to express it, but it is there. It's a presence, a void, a shadow of something that never fully materialized. I figure I don't know how to express or relay how I feel because I have never felt anything like this before.

It's as if I lost a part of me that I thought I would never loose. This elusive part of my soul, tied to you, has left an emptiness I can't seem to fill. I try to put it into words, but each attempt falls short, like trying to capture the wind in my hands. The feelings are there, raw and potent, yet they evade expression, slipping through my grasp.

I wonder if the reason I struggle to articulate these emotions is because they touch on a part of my heart that has never been touched before. It's unfamiliar territory, a landscape of uncharted emotions that leave me feeling both vulnerable and lost.

I guess love was just a word to you,
While to me, it was everything

Days's move slower now that you're gone.

What I would give to see what could have been. To witness the life and love we might have shared, now just a haunting memory of dreams unfulfilled. Every "what if" is a painful reminder of the future we lost, leaving me yearning for a reality that will never be

Sometimes, I'd rather be six feet under than
to bask in the what-ifs of our shortened love.

I often wonder if romantic love is designed to leave me in despair, forever questioning its reality. It feels like a cruel illusion, a tantalizing dream that always slips through my fingers just when I think I have it. I chase after it, hoping to capture its magic, only to be left with the bitter taste of disappointment. Is it truly real, or is it a figment of my imagination, a construct to keep me yearning and unfulfilled? The more I search for answers, the more elusive it becomes, leaving me to ponder if I am destined to chase an unattainable fantasy forever.

I thought I had escaped the thoughts of you until I found myself at a French bakery, thinking of you. It took everything not to break down. The pain returned, knowing that ultimately, you valued your comfort more than you valued me and what we built. Did you ever actually love me, or just the idea of what we had? I don't want to come back, but I can't help it. Why am I holding on to what could have been?

Maybe I have to feel this pain in order to heal from it. Perhaps enduring the heartache is the only way to truly move forward, to find a path that exists without you.

Seeing you again was a difficult but necessary decision. It brought to light the painful truth that we could never truly work. Without your father's acceptance, you would never be mine. Watching your father refuse to speak to me, knowing I would never earn his approval, was a harsh reality I had to face. You would always seek his approval, even when he is blinded by his own biases. It breaks my heart to realize that no matter how much we love each other, you will always choose him over us. His disapproval casts a shadow over our happiness, making it impossible for us to be together fully and freely. This realization is a wound that cuts deep, leaving me to grapple with a love that can never fully be.

I'm doing this to myself.

I need to learn to live without you, knowing that the ghost of you will be all there ever is. Your absence haunts me, but I must find a way to move forward, even with the lingering shadows of what once was.

Each day, I face the reality that some loves are not meant to last. They come into our lives to teach us, to shape us, and then leave us stronger than before. In your absence, I'm learning the importance of letting go, and also understanding the lessons I was meant to learn.

I find love fascinating. I curse it one moment but long for it the next. Love is the one thing that, no matter how much pain it has brought me, I will endlessly search for it. Does this make me insane or hopeful? Where is the line drawn?

I am hopeful that one day this void will be filled, and I will allow myself to seek love again. I cling to the belief that, with time, the wounds will heal, and the emptiness will be replaced by new possibilities. The ache in my heart will slowly fade, and the shadows of the past will no longer haunt me. One day, I will find the courage to open my heart once more, to embrace the chance for love and connection, and to trust that a brighter future awaits. Until then, I will nurture the hope that true healing and love are still within my grasp, even if it feels distant now.

As I walked down the stairwell of the coffeehouse, a tall, bearded, gentle-looking man uttered "excuse me, handsome" as we passed one another. In that moment, I realized the profound impact a stranger's words can have. For the first time, I felt seen in a way that didn't evoke fear but rather a sense of acceptance and love. It made me ponder how much of my life I had spent hiding from the world, afraid of judgment and rejection because of my experiences. Yet, in that brief exchange, I felt a warmth and validation that reminded me of the inherent worth we all possess, even if we sometimes forget it ourselves. It showed me that love can come from the simplest of gestures, and that being seen is a powerful form of love.

I'm finding value in those who have "loved" me and let their actions mold my mind into believing I am not worthy of love because that is what their actions showed me. Their inability to love me has been a harsh lesson, one that has often made me question my own worth.

But now, I'm starting to learn that their actions do not define me and never will. Their inability to love me is a result of the healing they have yet pursued. It is not a reflection of my value or my capacity to be loved. Their actions are mirrors of their own insecurities and unhealed wounds, not indicators of my worthiness.

As my understanding of love deepens, the world around me transforms from dull and gray to vibrant and full of color. I am noticing beauty I hadn't noticed before. I realize now that true love will come in its own time, when I am ready. That I don't need to worry.

Beyond the Mask

Section V: Dialogues with the Divine

Beyond the Mask

Abba,

Hard things are coming up, and I am trying to find joy in growth, but it is much harder than I thought. You have allowed me to walk through this for a purpose, and I am learning to lean on that. Please give me the strength to prevail through this; I know you're with me. Help me to see the lesson and apply it, allowing this experience to change me for the better. Help me to desire growth while also being content with where you have me. Help me to be more present and not so focused on the end result.

God,

Free me from myself, Please.

Abba,

I don't know how much more I have left in me. I'm trying to lean on You, but I keep failing. I have no energy; I just want my mind to be empty. I need You to take this burden from me. I feel like Job. I know You haven't abandoned me, but I can't bring myself to do what I know I need to, as it will only cause more problems. I fear the repercussions more than the fear itself.

I'm tired of explaining myself to people. Instead of offering empathy, they make me feel worse. I can't carry this anymore; it's taking too much of a toll. Please take this, Abba, I'm begging You. Give me the strength to endure, the peace to quiet my mind, and the faith to trust in Your plan even when I can't see a way forward.

Abba,

This is so difficult. The weight of making that call, after witnessing so much irresponsibility and immaturity around me, is crushing. It took everything in me to reach out in order to try to help them. Knowing the consequences and turmoil it would bring. The burden of these circumstances is becoming unbearable. I don't know what to do, and I'm not sure how much more I can take.

God,

I desperately need You to move. The stress and anxiety are consuming me; I fear for my sanity. Please provide me with a way out. I have tried on my own and have gotten nowhere. No matter how hard I try, I can't change other people or control their actions. This is something only You can do.

I am at my breaking point and need a miracle. Help me to find the strength to keep pushing forward, to trust in Your plan even when I can't see a way through. Give me peace in the midst of this chaos and the courage to face each day. Help me to see the purpose in this pain and to find growth in these trials

God,

I wish Your people would seek You as they should. If they did, everything could be so different.

God,

I am trying to think positively, and I'm trying to lean on You, but my mind keeps wandering. Lord, I need all of You. I know I'm not giving this my all, and I need to start. I am so tired of fighting this battle. I need to hand it over to You. This struggle is so much deeper and harder to handle than the assault I endured. I don't want to go through this alone. Please, take this burden from me and guide me through this darkness. I don't want to hold onto the pain any longer. I want it to just leave, I am trying to keep going but I am failing desperately. I want to feel your joy again, I know what I'm going through is going to glorify you. I'm just having a hard time seeing it.

I'm turning to other things again Abba, not as bad as before but it isn't what I should be doing but I still do it. I want to feel you in the way I did before all this pain. I need you more than ever, I'm at the end of myself. Thank you for listening to me. I love you Abba.

Oh sovereign, merciful Father,

How I long to see You face to face. How I yearn for the day when all sadness, trauma, and anger disappear for all eternity. How I long to be with You in Heaven. Help me to bring Your kingdom here on Earth. Give me the strength to focus on eternity now, knowing that the hope I desperately seek can only come from You.

Help me withstand the test of time, for I am so weak and easily distracted. Sanctify me, Father, and lead me. I want to glorify You in all that I do. I cast my worries to You and surrender my relationships into Your hands. Do as You please, for You see what I don't and hear what I can't. I trust in Your wisdom and guidance.

God,

How I need you. I am so weak, for in my own
strength I cannot beat this. I need your
strength to help me. I need to seek you
better when I am weak. I am beyond broken.
I know this next year is going to be hard, but
I know you wont leave my side. I will do my
best to stand by that truth. You are
preparing me for something great.

Abba,

Help transform this pain, fill the void only you can fill. I'm desperate.

Oh Lord, My God, My sovereign father,

I praise you for you didnt leave me stranded when I needed you the most. You hear me and guide me every step of the way. Thank you so much for sending Mark and placing him as my counselor. He has helped me in ways that will impact generations. He has helped show me that I am strong and can heal from the pain of the things of the past if I continue to press in. I am in utter awe of you Abba. I am learning to trust you more and more. Thank you for your provision, protection, love, mercy and forgiveness. I love you so much.

Father, I'm scared.

Please show me why.

"My son, you appreciate some of the most captivating and complex things I have created. I gave you the desire and love for these things, so you can see my love for you is so much deeper than these things"

"Now, please, appreciate the beauty and complexity you hold"

Worrying is such a peculiar and consuming thing. I have found that it prevents me from living life to its fullest potential. There are times when I think I may long for death, believing that only then will I be free from my earthly body and the constant burden of worry. God, please show me how to cherish life instead of yearning for its end. Help me to find peace in the present and to appreciate the beauty and opportunities that life offers. Teach me to release my worries and live more fully in Your grace.

Will my quest for fulfillment lead me to realize only God can fill this void?

God, help me find the beauty in the things
that bring me agony and despair.

Abba,

Your ways are mysterious yet marvelous beyond comprehension. You always reveal reason when needed and prepare me for everything in ways unfathomable to my mind. You use incalculable pain and evil to glorify Yourself in such a way that it can only point back to Your sovereign grace and mercy, which I could never earn.

You do not leave me stranded in the valley but use Your vessels to guide me through. You are in every tear, laugh, suicidal thought, sleepless night, joyful praise, silent suffering, and limitless celebration. You are the one constant that has and will continue to remain. For everything besides You will subside.

God,

 You've cleared my past and don't judge me
for it. Will I ever find someone who will see
me the same way?

Do the complexities of life draw us to You?
For your is simple yet vastly complex.
The simple calms, yet the complexities
challenge.
I'm learning there is bliss in experiencing
both.
We are made to be complex, yet we try to
make ourselves simpler.
For what? To minimize ourselves? To hide
who we truly are?
We should embrace our complexities, for
they are what make us who we are.

I often find myself asking the infamous question, "Why?" Answers rarely come as frequently as I'd prefer. Perhaps this is to protect me from truths I am not yet mature enough to handle or even fathom. Maybe it's because I am destined to seek the Creator when I ask this question. It's possible that this drives me to search deeper, and in doing so, I may become more comfortable with not always having the answer.

To live is to marvel in the beauty of the
creator.
To not know but to still wonder.
To adhere to the marvelous wonder which is
the mystery.
The mystery that keeps us alive.

My Dear Abba,

I'm starting to see You in everything, even in those who may not know You yet. I see You in the love of a Muslim, in the hope and joy of those who are part of the LGBTQ community. I see Your presence in the kindness of strangers and the beauty of nature. It's hard not to see You in everything around me. Sometimes, I just need to slow down and truly embrace it. Help me to remain open-hearted and to recognize Your love and grace in all people and moments. Guide me to be a vessel of Your love, spreading acceptance and compassion wherever I go.

Death has tried to take you over and over my son. Can you not see how special you are to me?

My Dear Jesus,

In my vast array of despair, I have begun to reflect on everything and am starting to see the beauty within it all. You allow beauty to exist in the darkest of places. In the midst of my pain, you reveal moments of grace and glimpses of hope. Through my tears, you show me the strength I never knew I had and the resilience that comes from faith. Even in my deepest sorrow, your love shines through, illuminating the path forward. Thank you for allowing me to see that even in the darkness, there is beauty and purpose.

Abba,

Thank you for not giving up on me, even
when I gave up on you.

Acknowledgments

Special thanks to my counselor, Mark, who believed in me and pushed me when things got tough. Our year together changed my life in ways I never imagined. Your support and insights guided me through the hardest moments, leading to personal growth and healing. I am eternally grateful for your gift and its impact on my life. I wouldn't be where I am now if it wasn't for you. Thank you from the bottom of my heart.

Special thanks to Pastor Jon for your leadership and love, which were instrumental in my journey toward healing after the assault. Because of you, I can now live in the forgiveness Jesus exemplifies. I am eternally grateful for each of you and the profound impact you've had on my life.

To my sister Ashlyn, thank you for embarking on this journey with me. Your honest feedback and judgment-free support mean the world to me. You are a blessing to everyone around you. I love you deeply and admire your love for literature and your desire to make a positive impact. Watching you grow into the incredible woman you are today has been a privilege. P.S. Dobby is now a free elf. I love you, sissy.

To my house church family, words cannot express how thankful I am for each of you. Your love and acceptance embody what it means to be Christ-centered. You have allowed me to be honest about my struggles, never leaving me stranded. Instead, you have built me up, ensuring I feel cared for and loved. Your unwavering support has been a beacon of hope, and I am profoundly grateful for the sense of belonging you have given me.

To James, you have shown me that I can reveal every part of myself and still be loved—something I didn't think was possible. Your unwavering support has been a beacon of hope and strength. Thank you for always believing in me, even when I struggled to believe in myself. Your willingness to have hard conversations has helped me grow and become a better person. You have always stood by my side, never wavering in your loyalty and friendship. Your presence has been a constant source of comfort and encouragement. You are truly a brother for life, and I am endlessly grateful for you. I love you, and I cherish the bond we share.

To Mladen and Rebecca, you're the older siblings I never had. You have constantly opened your home to me and guided me through life's craziest difficulties. Your unwavering support and love have provided me with a safe haven during turbulent times. I honestly wouldn't be here if God hadn't brought you into my life. I love you both more than words can express. Luka, Odie, and sometimes Hamilton (haha), you all hold a special place in my heart. Thank you for being my family and showing me the true meaning of unconditional love and support.